27 DAYS TO OVERCOMING DEPRESSION

27 DAYS TO OVERCOMING DEPRESSION

Debunking All The Lies

DONJIA M WALLS

J MERRILL

J Merrill Publishing, Inc.
434 Hillpine Drive
Columbus, OH 43207
www.JMerrill.pub

Paperback ISBN-13: *978-1-961475-36-6*
eBook ISBN-13: *978-1-7354280-3-1*

Book Title: 27 Days To Overcoming Depression: Debunking All The Lies
Author: Donjia M. Walls

Yahweh, I want to thank You for the constant prompting to share my story, because we overcome not only by the blood of the Lamb but by the word of our testimony.

To my husband, Bilah Walls, thank you for your unwavering support and encouragement. You gave me the extra push I needed not only to complete this book but to share it with the world.

To my firstborn, my son, Psalm Arye Walls and my unborn child—Mommy wants to thank you for being a consistent reminder of how essential I am to the generations that come after me.

To my discipler—also known as my spiritual father—Apostle Jeffrey Kearny, your spontaneity and challenges were invaluable during this process. Thank you for being honest, open, and transparent.

Finally, thank you to everyone who has supported or will support this book. My prayer for you is that you receive the tools you need for this journey.

—Donjia M. Walls

CONTENTS

FOREWORD

Many devotionals are written by authors who document what God can do, though they may never have truly experienced it. In contrast, Donjia records not just words but proof—she shares her lived experiences of God's presence and power. This is essential in a time that demands authenticity and truth. Donjia has achieved something rare: an actual devotional, not based on what she has heard about God, but on what she has personally encountered in Him.

Consider Thomas, who, despite the other disciples telling him they had seen Jesus—including the nail scars in His hands, feet, and side—remained unsatisfied until he saw it for himself. Likewise, Donjia offers the totality of her life experiences, both personal and in ministry, giving us a roadmap to recovery through devotion, faith-filled exercises, and prayer.

As you journey through this book, you'll find encouragement for your walk with God. Donjia acknowledges that discouragement can be part of the process but emphasizes that trust is essential. She introduces us to *The Joy of Suffering*, reminding us that Christ endured suffering for the joy set before Him. She encourages us to develop *Faith in the Wait* and to persevere even when walking through life's "Death Valley."

One of the key messages in this devotional is to *Know Your Weapons*. Donjia assures us that these spiritual tools are crucial in fighting the internal battles of condemnation and denial. She also invites us to reflect on the perspective offered by life: the rearview mirror is much smaller than the front windshield. Her command is clear—*Don't Go Back, Keep Working*.

These 27 devotions will inspire you to praise God during your most challenging times and to celebrate your victories. Prepare to be uplifted and encouraged.

Enjoy the journey.

~Apostle Jeffrey Kearny

DISCLAIMER

By engaging with this devotional, you acknowledge that Donjia M. Walls is not a licensed psychologist, therapist, or healthcare professional. This book is not intended to replace any form of treatment or care provided by licensed professionals qualified to diagnose and treat depression, anxiety, or other mental health conditions.

This devotional is not a substitute for psychological counseling, therapy, or medical advice. Instead, it is a personal account of what the Holy Spirit revealed to Donjia during her journey through depression. She shares the tools given to her—including scriptures, prayers, and exercises—that helped her along the way.

Please note that individual outcomes from reading and applying this devotional may vary. While these tools were transformative in Donjia's experience, no guarantee is made that the same results will occur for everyone. Her prayer is that you read, pray, and apply these principles daily, allowing the Holy Spirit to guide you through your own unique process of healing and overcoming.

One assurance remains: when we fully and sincerely submit ourselves to God, we can resist the devil, and he will flee (James 4:7).

INTRODUCTION

According to the *Cambridge Dictionary*, *overcoming* is defined as "to defeat or succeed in controlling or dealing with something."

Join me on this journey, led by the Holy Spirit, as I share how I overcame the battles of depression, anxiety, and suicidal thoughts.

DAY 1

MY THOUGHTS

"Finally, brethren, whatsoever things are true, whatsoever things are honest, whatsoever things are just, whatsoever things are pure, whatsoever things are lovely, whatsoever things are of good report; if there be any virtue, and if there be any praise, think on these things."

— PHILIPPIANS 4:8 (KJV)

DEVOTIONAL:

Have you ever noticed how much time you spend in your own thoughts? Or how easy it is to hold on to the negative narratives that replay in your mind? This is a common experience for many who battle depression. That's why I love how Paul tells us, as believers, what we *should* think about.

In Philippians, Paul reminds us that God will guard our hearts (Phil. 4:7), but it's our responsibility to direct our thoughts toward what pleases God—things that are true, honest, just, pure, lovely, and of good report (Phil. 4:8).

Notice that this scripture does not mention anything negative. This reassures me that when negative thoughts arise, I must recognize them but not dwell on or embrace them as truth, because they are not from God.

One technique I've drawn from this scripture, and still practice, is to align my thoughts with God's Word. For example, when the narrative "I am not good enough" plays in my mind, I ask myself, "Does this align with the Philippians standard of what I should be thinking about?"

Now, I turn the question to you. The narrative you hear may be different, but whatever it is, remember to recognize it without accepting it as your truth.

EXERCISE:

Commit Philippians 4:8 to memory. Whenever negative thoughts arise, compare them to this verse. Deny the thoughts that don't align with what is true, honest, just, pure, lovely, or of good report.

PRAYER:

Father, help me to understand that with You guarding my heart, as promised in Philippians 4:7, I must keep my mind focused on the things Paul charges us to think about in Philippians 4:8. I know some days will be easier than others, but I decree and declare that this practice will become a lifestyle—not only for me but for the generations to come. In Jesus' mighty name, Amen.

REFLECTIONS:

_____

_____

_____

_____

_____

_____

_____

_____

_____

_____

_____

_____

_____

_____

_____

_____

_____

_____

_____

_____

_____

DAY 2
DISCOURAGEMENT

"And the Lord, he it is that doth go before thee; he will be with thee, he will not fail thee, neither forsake thee: fear not, neither be dismayed."

— DEUTERONOMY 31:8 (KJV)

DEVOTIONAL:

Have you ever experienced discouragement? If so, do you know what triggered it? Discouragement is defined as a loss of confidence, enthusiasm, or a sense of disheartenment.

Often, discouragement arises from feelings of inadequacy, unworthiness, or a belief that we aren't qualified for the task Yahweh has given us. When we truly examine these moments, we often find that discouragement stems from comparing our process or outcomes to those of others.

The danger in comparison lies in forgetting that Yahweh has uniquely designed each of our journeys. We might find ourselves saying, "I don't do it like them," or "People won't receive from me." Such thoughts can spiral into deeper feelings of discouragement and even depression.

Deuteronomy 31:8 reminds us that the Lord Himself goes before us. He will not fail us, nor will He forsake us. If Yahweh has called us to something, He will see us through it. Let this scripture be your anchor in moments of discouragement, reminding you that you don't walk this path alone.

EXERCISE:

Commit Deuteronomy 31:8 to memory. When discouragement arises, repeat this verse to remind yourself that Yahweh is leading you and will ensure your victory.

PRAYER:

Father, I thank You today. I confess that I often feel discouraged, especially when I compare my calling to others or when I place expectations on people who have let me down. Help me to embody the truth of Deuteronomy 31:8 so I can stand firm and overcome these feelings. I declare it done. In Jesus' mighty name, Amen.

DONJIA M WALLS

REFLECTIONS:

_____

_____

_____

_____

_____

_____

_____

_____

_____

_____

_____

_____

_____

_____

_____

_____

_____

_____

_____

_____

_____

DAY 3

THE CRY OUT

"The righteous cry, and the Lord heareth, and delivereth them out of all their troubles."

— PSALM 34:17 (KJV)

DEVOTIONAL:

This scripture has been pivotal for me, serving as a foundation for proper alignment and for the real work of healing to begin. For myself—and for others I know who have faced or are facing depression—it often brings silence. Depression can lead us to say nothing about what's happening inside us, isolating us in a way that aligns with the enemy's agenda.

The goal of the enemy through depression is to make us suffer in silence. Not only does this silence separate us from those around us, but it can also distance us from Yahweh, the One who knows all. This silence often grows into lies about our feelings, emotions, and thoughts.

Psalm 34:17 reminds us that when we cry out, the Lord hears us and delivers us. Since God's Word is true, it's clear why the enemy works so hard to convince us that no one hears us or cares. The longer we remain silent, the longer we delay our deliverance.

We must put aside our pride, shame, and fear and cry out to Yahweh. When we do, He hears and takes action. Crying out is not a sign of weakness but a step toward healing and revelation.

EXERCISE:

Commit Psalm 34:17 to memory. Challenge yourself to release what's inside and cry out to Yahweh so He can hear and deliver you. Additionally, find someone you can speak with—whether a therapist, pastor, mentor, or trusted friend—so you have accountability and consistent check-ins.

PRAYER:

Father, I thank You for today and for Your Word, which is alive and true. Thank You for Psalm 34:17, which reminds me that I can cry out to You and that You not only hear me but also deliver me. You are a God who is both able and willing. Give me courage beyond my shame to cry out and receive healing. Lead me to trustworthy individuals who can hold me accountable so I am no longer silent. In Jesus' mighty name, Amen.

REFLECTIONS:

_____

_____

_____

_____

_____

_____

_____

_____

_____

_____

_____

_____

_____

_____

_____

_____

_____

_____

_____

_____

_____

_____

_____

DAY 4
TRUST IS A MUST

"Many sorrows shall be to the wicked; but he who trusts in the Lord, mercy shall surround him."

— PSALM 32:10 (NKJV)

DEVOTIONAL:

What do you place your trust in? Money, relationships, a job, family, friends, future goals? Trust is defined as a firm belief in the reliability, truth, ability, or strength of someone or something. With this in mind, ask yourself, *Do I truly trust God?*

This scripture reminds us that trusting in the Lord brings the blessing of His mercy surrounding us. On the other hand, without trust, we are left with sorrows. But what does this have to do with depression? I'm glad you asked.

I realized that when I didn't fully trust God, it amplified my depression. The things I placed my trust in— things like people or plans—would inevitably fail me, leaving me feeling empty and disappointed. For change and healing to occur, *trust is a must.*

We cannot limit what God wants to do in and through us because of our inability to trust Him. Not only is He able to meet our needs, but He is more than willing to do so. Let's take a step forward and choose to trust Him fully.

EXERCISE:

Commit Psalm 32:10 to memory. Then, write two lists (be honest):
1. The things you currently put your trust in.
2. The areas in your life where you don't fully trust God.
Once you've completed your lists, confess these things out loud to God and ask Him for the grace to trust Him completely.

PRAYER:

Father, I thank You for speaking to me today through Psalm 32:10. You've shown me that trusting in You allows me to experience Your mercy in fullness. I confess that my lack of trust in certain areas has caused voids in my life. Help me, Yahweh, to trust You fully—not just in some areas but in all areas of my life. I declare it done. In Jesus' mighty name, Amen.

REFLECTIONS:

_____

_____

_____

_____

_____

_____

_____

_____

_____

_____

_____

_____

_____

_____

_____

_____

_____

_____

_____

_____

_____

_____

DAY 5

IN DUE TIME

"Therefore humble yourselves under the mighty hand of God, that He may exalt you in due time, casting all your care upon Him, for He cares for you."

— 1 PETER 5:6–7 (NKJV)

DEVOTIONAL:

In my journey of faith, I've learned that planning can sometimes lead to disappointment. While I love to plan, I realized that much of my planning stemmed from a desire to control situations. Can you relate to that?

Let me clarify—I'm not saying planning is bad. In fact, our Heavenly Father operates with decency and order (1 Corinthians 14:40). However, we must examine the *heart* behind our planning. Just because something seems good doesn't mean it's from God.

In 1 Peter 5:6–7, we are called to humble ourselves under God's mighty hand. This means submitting to His will and His ways for our lives. When we do this, the scripture promises that God will exalt us *in due time*.

The phrase "in due time" caught my attention. According to Webster's Dictionary, *in due time* is an idiom meaning "eventually, at the appropriate time." Yahweh intentionally included this phrase to remind us that our exaltation will come at the time He deems appropriate.

This led me to Ecclesiastes 3, which reminds us that there is a time for everything under heaven (Ecclesiastes 3:1–8). The key takeaway is that we must not force or operate outside of Yahweh's timing, as doing so only creates unnecessary difficulty.

EXERCISE:

Commit 1 Peter 5:6–7 to memory. Write down all your plans and ideas for your life. Then, reflect on how many of these plans include God and how many truly originated from Him.

PRAYER:

Father, I thank You for Your Word today. I'm grateful for the reminder that there is a time and place for everything according to Your will. Help me not to function outside of Your timing but to rest in Your due time. Teach me to humble myself and submit fully to Your plans for my life. In Jesus' mighty name, Amen.

DONJIA M WALLS

REFLECTIONS:

_____

_____

_____

_____

_____

_____

_____

_____

_____

_____

_____

_____

_____

_____

_____

_____

_____

_____

_____

_____

_____

DAY 6

WHO'S IN TROUBLE?

"These things I have spoken unto you, that in me ye might have peace. In the world ye shall have tribulation: but be of good cheer; I have overcome the world."

— JOHN 16:33 (KJV)

DEVOTIONAL:

In John 16, Jesus speaks to His disciples, preparing them for what is to come and demonstrating His knowledge and wisdom. The disciples admit they now understand Him because He is speaking plainly, not figuratively (John 16:29).

In verse 33, Jesus offers a powerful assurance: while the world will bring sorrows and troubles, they can have peace in Him because He has overcome the world.

This truth brings me so much comfort. Knowing that Christ's work on the cross has already conquered the very things that try to overwhelm me fills me with peace. When I feel consumed by the cares, worries, fears, and weight of this world, I recite John 16:33 to remind myself that Jesus has succeeded in dealing with all of it. My role is to release those burdens and give them to Him to handle.

EXERCISE:

Commit John 16:33 to memory. Then, make a list of the things that typically overwhelm you—no matter how long it is. Once you've completed the list, go through each item one by one. Cross it out and write next to it: "Jesus has overcome this" or "Jesus has succeeded in dealing with this."

PRAYER:

Father, I thank You for Your Word today. Help me to remember, in moments when I feel overwhelmed or burdened by this world, that You have already overcome it all. Strengthen my faith so I can fully believe and stand on this truth. In Jesus' mighty name, Amen.

REFLECTIONS:

DAY 7

ALL THE THINGS

"For I am persuaded that neither death nor life, nor angels nor principalities nor powers, nor things present nor things to come, nor height nor depth, nor any other created thing, shall be able to separate us from the love of God which is in Christ Jesus our Lord."

— ROMANS 8:38–39 (NKJV)

DEVOTIONAL:

Have you ever reached a point where life felt overwhelming? Has the weight of the world made you feel distant from God? Let me remind you, according to Romans 8:38–39, that nothing can separate us from His love.

Paul's words in this scripture are some of the most encouraging statements for us as believers. He emphasizes that no matter what we face, none of it can separate us from the love of Christ for those who are truly in Him. Paul highlights two extremes—death and life—and lists many other things as well.

Let's focus on death. Death is often seen as the ultimate separator, cutting us off from everything and everyone. Yet Paul assures us that not even death can separate us from God's love. That speaks volumes.

In my darkest moments—when I was battling depression, suicidal thoughts, and even surviving suicide attempts—I remember God reminding me of the blood Jesus shed for me. That alone became reason enough to keep living.

Today, let's hold fast to this truth: no matter what tries to separate you, no matter what whispers lie to you about God's love, know for certain that those are false. God's love is unshakable and unwavering for those who are in Christ.

EXERCISE:

Commit Romans 8:38–39 to memory. Each time you feel distant from God or hear the lie that He doesn't love you, recite this scripture to combat that thought.

PRAYER:

Father, I thank You for Your Word today. I confess that there are times when I hear a narrative in my mind telling me that You don't love me because of what I've done or what I've been through. Help me to fully grasp that for those who are in Christ, nothing can separate us from Your love. Give me the strength to fully submit and surrender everything to You so I can live a life that pleases You. In Jesus' mighty name, Amen.

REFLECTIONS:

_____

_____

_____

_____

_____

_____

_____

_____

_____

_____

_____

_____

_____

_____

_____

_____

_____

_____

DAY 8

HE COMFORTS, WE COMFORT

"Blessed be the God and Father of our Lord Jesus Christ, the Father of mercies and God of all comfort, who comforts us in all our tribulation, that we may be able to comfort those who are in any trouble, with the comfort with which we ourselves are comforted by God."

— 2 CORINTHIANS 1:3–4 (NKJV)

DEVOTIONAL:

According to *Webster's Dictionary*, *comfort* means "to give strength and hope to" or "to ease the grief or trouble of." Comfort is also a verb, making it an action word.

In 2 Corinthians 1:3–4, God reveals Himself as the God of all comfort, who strengthens and sustains us in our troubles. If we truly reflect on it, we'll see that even in our lowest, most depressed moments, it is God who pulls us through. We cannot overcome these moments on our own—it is His comfort that carries us.

Verse 4 takes this truth a step further. God doesn't comfort us just to bring us to the other side of our struggles. He comforts us so we can, in turn, extend comfort to others.

This scripture is part of the reason I knew I had to create this devotional. It's a charge from God to share my testimony and extend the comfort He has given me. So, the next time you experience the God of all comfort, remember that you're also called to pay it forward by comforting someone else in their time of need.

EXERCISE:

Commit 2 Corinthians 1:3–4 to memory. Pray and ask God to reveal someone in your life who needs comfort. Then, seek His guidance on how to offer that comfort to them.

PRAYER:

Father, I thank You for Your Word today. I acknowledge You as the God of all comfort and praise You for that attribute. Teach me to fully understand and practice comforting others as You have comforted me. In Jesus' mighty name, Amen.

REFLECTIONS:

_____

_____

_____

_____

_____

_____

_____

_____

_____

_____

_____

_____

_____

_____

_____

_____

_____

_____

_____

_____

_____

_____

_____

DAY 9

THE JOY IN SUFFERING

"Beloved, do not think it strange concerning the fiery trial which is to try you, as though some strange thing happened to you; but rejoice to the extent that you partake of Christ's sufferings, that when His glory is revealed, you may also be glad with exceeding joy."

— 1 PETER 4:12–13 (NKJV)

DEVOTIONAL:

According to *Webster's Dictionary*, to *suffer* means "to submit to or be forced to endure." Suffering is not a concept most of us want to embrace. In fact, the idea of suffering with joy can feel almost impossible.

In 1 Peter 4:12–13, Peter reminds us that as followers of Christ, we will face trials and difficulties. These challenges are meant to purge us of self-reliance and lead us toward total trust in Jesus. Peter urges us not to be surprised by suffering but to rejoice in it.

This truth was difficult for me to accept because, like most, I didn't want to suffer. Who does? But then I was reminded of Mark 8:34–35, where Jesus tells us that we must take up our cross to follow Him.

When we consider what Christ endured on the cross, we see a picture of ultimate suffering. Yet, His suffering had purpose and brought victory. Similarly, though suffering isn't a popular or comfortable experience, it is a necessary one.

In moments of darkness, depression, sadness, or hardship, we must pray for the strength to find joy in the midst of our trials. This isn't optional—it's a command for believers, and it transforms how we endure.

EXERCISE:

Commit 1 Peter 4:12–13 to memory. Identify a healthy activity that brings you joy—such as writing, painting, listening to music, driving, or walking. Incorporate this activity into your weekly routine. Aim to do it once or twice a week and journal about any emotional shifts you experience.

PRAYER:

Father God, I thank You for Your Word today. It is alive and working for my good. I pray that You help me understand and practice the concept of finding joy in suffering. In moments when I feel helpless, remind me that You and the Holy Spirit are with me. Teach me to trust You completely, even in the hardest times. In Jesus' mighty name, Amen.

REFLECTIONS:

_____

_____

_____

_____

_____

_____

_____

_____

_____

_____

_____

_____

_____

_____

_____

_____

_____

_____

_____

_____

_____

_____

DAY 10
FROM CRYING TO DANCING

"You have turned my mourning into joyful dancing. You have taken away my clothes of mourning and clothed me with joy."

— PSALM 30:11 (NLT)

DEVOTIONAL:

Have you ever thought about mourning as something you wear? What would an outfit of mourning look like? Traditionally, mourning is associated with black clothing—a visible expression of deep sorrow.

In this scripture, David acknowledges that God has answered his prayer for forgiveness, turning his mourning into dancing, or gladness. So, here's a reflective question for today: *What are we still wearing because we haven't fully embraced the forgiveness of God?*

The King James Version (KJV) of this verse specifically mentions sackcloth. Sackcloth, a rough garment made from goat's hair, was worn as a visual sign of mourning during biblical times. Its coarse texture served as a constant, uncomfortable reminder of tragedy.

Similarly, when we "wear" depression, anxiety, sadness, overthinking, or worry, they become reminders of the struggles and pain that brought them into our lives. To shed these garments of mourning, we must embrace the forgiveness and love of God. When we do, it changes not only our hearts but our attitudes about who we are and whose we are.

EXERCISE:

Commit Psalm 30:11 to memory. Write down the emotional "clothing" you've been wearing—worry, fear, shame, guilt, doubt, or anything else. Ask God to guide you in embracing His forgiveness so you can strip off these layers and continue your journey of overcoming.

PRAYER:

Father God, I thank You for Your Word today. I first ask for Your forgiveness for all sins I've committed, both knowingly and unknowingly, against You. Reveal to me any people, places, situations, or things I need to forgive so that I can align with Your Word in Matthew 6:14–15, which reminds me that I must forgive to be forgiven. Help me to take off these garments of mourning I've been wearing, whether knowingly or unknowingly. I desire to step into the joy You provide. I cannot do this without You. Help me, Lord. In Jesus' mighty name, Amen.

REFLECTIONS:

_____

_____

_____

_____

_____

_____

_____

_____

_____

_____

_____

_____

_____

_____

_____

_____

_____

_____

_____

_____

_____

_____

DAY 11

FAINT IN THE WAIT

"But those who trust in the Lord will find new strength. They will soar high on wings like eagles. They will run and not grow weary. They will walk and not faint."

— ISAIAH 40:31 (NLT)

DEVOTIONAL:

What does your waiting look like? Are you busy waiting? Sad waiting? Angry waiting? Take a moment to reflect on this: *How am I waiting?* This is a critical factor to consider in our spiritual journey.

In Isaiah 40:31, the prophet provides encouragement to the Israelites after warning them about their impending exile by the Babylonians. At this point, they were in despair and questioning their faith. This is where Isaiah's powerful words offer hope and perspective.

Let's break this scripture down to grasp its depth:

• *"Those who trust in the Lord"*

The Israelites were called to place their trust in God while awaiting deliverance. Similarly, we are reminded to trust God during times of uncertainty and despair.

• *"Will find new strength"*

This is a promise of restoration. In our waiting, God renews our strength, enabling us to withstand our circumstances.

• *"They will soar high on wings like eagles"*

Eagles symbolize ease, grace, and confidence. This metaphor reassures us that through Christ, we will rise above our obstacles with strength and assurance.

• *"They will run and not grow weary"*

Isaiah encourages endurance, reminding us that God equips us to maintain momentum even in adversity.

• *"They will walk and not faint"*

With God, we can continue forward on our journey without losing hope or strength.

This scripture invites us to adopt a posture of trust and confidence in God's timing, no matter how challenging the waiting may feel.

EXERCISE:

Commit Isaiah 40:31 to memory. Reflect on each part of the verse and write down what it personally means to you. Consider how these promises apply to your current season of waiting.

PRAYER:

Father, I thank You for Your Word today. Teach me how to wait well in every season of my life. Help me to trust You fully, knowing that You renew my strength and keep me steadfast. Let me be encouraged by Your promises and reminded of Your faithfulness as I rely on You. In Jesus' mighty name, Amen.

REFLECTIONS:

_____

_____

_____

_____

_____

_____

_____

_____

_____

_____

_____

_____

_____

_____

_____

_____

_____

_____

_____

DAY 12
IDENTIFY THE PURPOSE

"The thief's purpose is to steal and kill and destroy. My purpose is to give them a rich and satisfying life."

— JOHN 10:10 (NLT)

DEVOTIONAL:

Identifying the voice, purposes, and plans of God can sometimes feel challenging, especially if we don't fully know His Word or His character. John 10:10 makes the distinction clear: the thief's purpose is to steal, kill, and destroy, while God's purpose is to give us a rich and satisfying life.

I love how this translation uses the word *purpose*. When the Holy Spirit led me to this scripture, I reflected on the question: *What is the purpose of depression?* That question helped me identify the true source of depression. Nothing I experienced in a depressive state reflected the rich and satisfying life God promises, so I knew it wasn't from Him.

This verse challenged me to evaluate the thoughts and circumstances in my life that were stealing, killing, and destroying me. It also motivated me to learn about God's character and all that He is.

We must remember that God's desire for us is to live abundantly, as the King James Version says: "I am come that they might have life, and that they might have it more abundantly." To experience this, we need to fully submit to and commit ourselves to Him.

EXERCISE:

Commit John 10:10 to memory. Research the names of God (e.g., Jehovah Jireh, Jehovah Shalom) and create a visible list to help you learn and identify His characteristics.

PRAYER:

Dear Heavenly Father, I thank You for Your Word today. Thank You for teaching me how to distinguish between Your purposes and the plans of the enemy. According to Jeremiah 29:11, Your plans for me are to prosper me and not to harm me. If something isn't bringing me life and abundance, it likely isn't from You. Help me to grow in understanding and trust in You. In Jesus' mighty name, Amen.

DONJIA M WALLS

REFLECTIONS:

_____

_____

_____

_____

_____

_____

_____

_____

_____

_____

_____

_____

_____

_____

_____

_____

_____

_____

_____

_____

_____

_____

_____

DAY 13

THE BEST REST

"Come to me, all who labor and are heavy laden, and I will give you rest."

— MATTHEW 11:28 (ESV)

DEVOTIONAL:

Have you ever read or heard a scripture that didn't fully resonate with you until you faced a specific situation? For me, Matthew 11:28 was one of those scriptures. I'd heard it countless times in the King James Version and the New Living Translation, but the English Standard Version introduced a word I wasn't as familiar with: *laden*.

The verse says: "Come to me, all who labor and are heavy laden, and I will give you rest." Let's break it down by focusing on three key words: *labor, laden,* and *rest.*
- *Laden* is defined as "heavily loaded or weighed down."
- *Labor* means "work, especially hard physical work."
- *Rest* is "to cease work or movement in order to relax, refresh oneself, or recover strength."

Now, plugging these definitions into the verse can help us connect more deeply:

"Come to me, all who do hard physical work and are heavily loaded or weighed down, and I will give you the ability to cease work or movement in order to relax, refresh yourself, or recover strength."

This verse reminds us that it isn't God's desire for us to operate in our own strength. He understands the physical, mental, emotional, and spiritual strain we endure. Even when we overwork ourselves to escape feelings of depression or anxiety, God offers us rest. Let this scripture be a reminder to rely on the One who grants true rest and renewal.

EXERCISE:

Commit Matthew 11:28 to memory. Set aside intentional time to rest at least one day each week, even if it's just for an hour or two. Schedule it and ask someone to hold you accountable.

PRAYER:

Father, I thank You for Your Word, which is alive and active in my life. I ask for Your help in embracing rest. I confess that at times I take on too much in an attempt to override the heaviness I feel, but it only adds more weight. Today, I cast all my cares on You because You care for me. Grant me rest in every area of my life. In Jesus' mighty name, Amen.

REFLECTIONS:

_____

_____

_____

_____

_____

_____

_____

_____

_____

_____

_____

_____

_____

_____

_____

_____

_____

_____

_____

DAY 14

ALL YOUR

"Trust in the Lord with all thine heart; and lean not unto thine own understanding. In all thy ways acknowledge him, and he shall direct thy paths."

— PROVERBS 3:5–6 (KJV)

DEVOTIONAL:

Today's verses from Proverbs are widely recognized and deeply impactful. The world often promotes the idea that we are fully capable of "handling anything that comes our way" on our own. Many of the methods and philosophies we are encouraged to follow leave God completely out of the equation.

As children of God, we are called to put our trust in Him, not in the ways of the world (Psalm 20:7). Proverbs 3:5 emphasizes trusting the Lord with all our heart. The word *heart* is referenced 826 times in the King James Bible, according to *Strong's Exhaustive Concordance of the Bible.*

Why does God place such importance on the heart? The heart is the center of spiritual activity and human life. Romans 2:15 reveals that the heart is the seat of our conscience, meaning it acts as an inner guide, helping us discern right from wrong. Trusting God with all our heart is not just a suggestion—it's an essential part of our spiritual journey, guiding us to align our thoughts, actions, and decisions with His will.

EXERCISE:

Commit Proverbs 3:5–6 to memory. Spend 5–10 minutes today doing a heart check: reflect on your feelings, thoughts, and motives, and ask God to reveal areas where you need to trust Him more.

PRAYER:

Father, thank You for Your Word, which is alive and working in every part of our lives. Today, we pray Psalm 139:23–24: "Search me, O God, and know my heart; try me, and know my thoughts. And see if there be any wicked way in me, and lead me in the way everlasting." In Jesus' mighty name, Amen.

REFLECTIONS:

_____

_____

_____

_____

_____

_____

_____

_____

_____

_____

_____

_____

_____

_____

_____

_____

_____

_____

_____

_____

_____

_____

DAY 15

DEATH VALLEY

"Even when I walk through the darkest valley, I will not be afraid, for you are close beside me. Your rod and your staff protect and comfort me."

— PSALM 23:4 (NLT)

DEVOTIONAL:

During a challenging period, King David wrote Psalm 23. In verse 4, he declares his confidence in God's presence and care: "Even when I walk through the darkest valley, I will not be afraid, for you are close beside me. Your rod and your staff protect and comfort me."

The "rod" was a tool shepherds used to protect their sheep from predators, while the "staff" was used to guide and direct the flock. With this understanding, we can rephrase the latter part of the verse: "Your correction, discipline, guidance, and defense protect and comfort me."

David understood what many of us are striving to grasp more deeply each day: even in our darkest times, it is God's very nature—His guidance, discipline, protection, and care—that carries us through. These two instruments symbolize God's active role in leading us, protecting us, and providing for us. They remind us that God is always present, watching over us, even when we feel surrounded by life's "dark valleys."

EXERCISE:

Commit Psalm 23:4 to memory. When faced with challenges or uncertainties, make a conscious decision to trust in God's presence and guidance rather than succumbing to fear or anxiety. Repeat scriptural truths to yourself, engage in worship, and reflect on God's unchanging character and promises.

PRAYER:

Lord, I adore You and Your unending love for me. I confess that I often let fear take hold during difficult times. Thank You for Your constant presence, guidance, and care. Help me to trust in You, even in the darkest moments of life. May Your rod and staff comfort and assure me, and may I always remember that I am never alone. In Jesus' name, Amen.

REFLECTIONS:

_____

_____

_____

_____

_____

_____

_____

_____

_____

_____

_____

_____

_____

_____

_____

_____

_____

_____

_____

_____

_____

_____

_____

DAY 16

IS IT MORNING YET?

"For his anger endureth but a moment; in his favour is life: weeping may endure for a night, but joy cometh in the morning."

— PSALM 30:5 (KJV)

DEVOTIONAL:

Have you ever gone to bed eagerly anticipating the morning because of a trip or an adventure, only to wake up and realize it was still night? Sometimes you might welcome the extra sleep, while other times it feels like the night will never end.

This verse is often quoted in church, but in my darkest seasons, I questioned if morning would ever come. I asked God, "What is night, and what is morning?" His response reshaped my understanding. He revealed that night and morning are not confined to a 24-hour cycle.

God showed me that night represents the darkest times in our lives, while morning is the moment we allow His light to break through. He said, "Weeping will continue as long as you welcome and embrace darkness, but joy will break through when you are ready for Me to shine light on all the dark places."

This insight challenged me. The next time you feel stuck in a prolonged season of darkness, reflect on whether there are areas of your life where you haven't allowed God's light to shine. Remember, morning can come at any time—don't miss it by waiting for a physical sunrise when God is ready to illuminate your life now.

EXERCISE:

Commit Psalm 30:5 to memory. Reflect on the areas of your life that feel like "dark" places. As you identify them, declare Psalm 18:28 over each one:

"For it is you who light my lamp; the Lord my God lightens my darkness."

PRAYER:

Father, I thank You for Your Word and the revelation of night and morning. I declare that You are the morning I seek. Forgive me for waiting for false mornings in people, places, and things. Help me to stop dwelling in the darkness and to embrace the light You offer. In Jesus' mighty name, Amen.

REFLECTIONS:

_____

_____

_____

_____

_____

_____

_____

_____

_____

_____

_____

_____

_____

_____

_____

_____

_____

_____

_____

_____

DAY 17

HONESTY IS THE BEST POLICY

"Hear me speedily, O Lord: my spirit faileth: hide not thy face from me, lest I be like unto them that go down into the pit. Cause me to hear thy lovingkindness in the morning; for in thee do I trust: cause me to know the way wherein I should walk; for I lift up my soul unto thee. Deliver me, O Lord, from mine enemies: I flee unto thee to hide me."

— PSALM 143:7–9 (KJV)

DEVOTIONAL:

Most of the Psalms were written by David, and many reflect his raw emotions—joy, sorrow, and despair. Psalm 143 is a heartfelt prayer from David to God, and verse 7 stood out to me during a dark season in my life.

God brought something to my attention through this verse: the importance of truth. I had to be honest with myself, those around me, and most importantly, with God.

David has an incredible way of presenting his flaws and faults to God with humility and self-awareness. He acknowledges that his flesh fails and fully relies on God for strength and direction. Embracing this truth—that I could not and should not rely on my flesh—was transformative for me.

I also realized there were other truths about myself that I hadn't addressed. I had to ask God to reveal these areas so He could heal them.

Honesty with God isn't about shame or guilt; it's about letting Him into the broken places so He can restore and renew us.

EXERCISE:

Commit Psalm 143:7–9 to memory. Write or text a prayer to God, being completely honest about your flaws and faults. Lay everything before Him with humility and trust.

PRAYER:

Use the prayer you wrote/texted as your personal conversation with God.

REFLECTIONS:

_____

_____

_____

_____

_____

_____

_____

_____

_____

_____

_____

_____

_____

_____

_____

_____

_____

_____

_____

_____

_____

DAY 18

IF YOU HAVE PLANS, CANCEL THEM!

"For I know the thoughts that I think toward you, saith the Lord, thoughts of peace, and not of evil, to give you an expected end."

— JEREMIAH 29:11 (KJV)

DEVOTIONAL:

Let me first challenge you to memorize Jeremiah 29:11 if you haven't already.

Are you a planner like me? I love having things organized, prepared, and ready to go. But something I've learned—sometimes slowly, sometimes quickly—is that this mindset doesn't always align with how God operates.

God has a plan for *all* of us, yet we often create our own plans and then bring them to Him, expecting His stamp of approval. Jeremiah 29:11 reminds us that *God knows what He is doing,* and our job is to trust Him and follow His lead.

I'm not saying that planning is bad—far from it! God values stewardship and preparation. However, we must be cautious not to plan *against* His will, whether consciously or unconsciously. When we align ourselves with God's plans, we experience His joy, peace, and provision. It's when we go against the flow of His purpose that our journey becomes unnecessarily difficult.

Let's commit today to submit our plans to Him and embrace His perfect design for our lives.

EXERCISE:

Commit Jeremiah 29:11 to memory. Write down your plans for your life, then take time to submit them to God in prayer. Ask Him to reveal whether your plans align with His will.

PRAYER:

Abba, I thank You for thinking so highly of me that You created a plan for my life from the foundation of the world. Help me to surrender every plan I have that does not align with Your will. Forgive me for exalting my own ideas and ambitions above You. Today, I declare with my heart that Your plan takes priority over everything else. In the mighty and matchless name of Jesus Christ, Amen.

REFLECTIONS:

_____

_____

_____

_____

_____

_____

_____

_____

_____

_____

_____

_____

_____

_____

_____

_____

_____

_____

_____

_____

DAY 19

WHAT IS THE COMMAND?

"Have not I commanded thee? Be strong and of a good courage; be not afraid, neither be thou dismayed: for the Lord thy God is with thee whithersoever thou goest."

— JOSHUA 1:9 (KJV)

DEVOTIONAL:

Joshua 1:1–9 is known as God's commission to Joshua. For me, verse 9 has been particularly convicting. Too often, I've forgotten what God has spoken to me and who He has called me to be.

Much of the depression and anxiety I've experienced stemmed from struggling with my identity. Growing up, I didn't see myself reflected in the world's standards of beauty. I often felt like an outcast, disconnected from society. I now realize that this feeling of being "set apart" aligns with God's truth in John 17:11. As His children, we are in the world, but not of it.

God has placed a mandate on the lives of His children. If you identify as His, this applies to you too. Admittedly, it can be difficult to live in a world that constantly tries to shape us through social media, entertainment, and societal norms. However, we are called to do, say, give, write, sing, or create what God has purposed for us, even when it sets us apart.

Joshua 1:9 reminds us of God's command to be strong, courageous, unafraid, and undismayed because He is with us wherever we go. Let this verse encourage you to step boldly into who God has called you to be.

EXERCISE:

Commit Joshua 1:9 to memory. Look up the definitions of *strong, good courage, afraid,* and *dismayed.* Once you've defined them, substitute their meanings into the scripture and read it aloud to reinforce God's command in your heart.

PRAYER:

Dear Heavenly Father, thank You for the command of Your Word. Show me what it looks like to have strength, courage, and confidence in You, and to live without fear or dismay. Help me to obey Your command, even when it causes me to stand out in the world. I declare these things done in Jesus' mighty name, Amen.

REFLECTIONS:

_____

_____

_____

_____

_____

_____

_____

_____

_____

_____

_____

_____

_____

_____

_____

_____

_____

_____

_____

_____

_____

DAY 20

TURN ON THE LIGHT!

"Then spake Jesus again unto them, saying, I am the light of the world: he that followeth me shall not walk in darkness, but shall have the light of life."
- PSALM 119:105 (KJV)

"Thy word is a lamp unto my feet, and a light unto my path."
- JOHN 8:12 (KJV)

DEVOTIONAL:

Say this out loud: *"Holy Spirit, help me turn on my light!"* How do you feel? That's our focus for today, so we're starting with intention.

After spending time reflecting on darkness, it's time to shine light into every dark place in our lives. *Light,* as defined by the dictionary, is a natural agent that stimulates sight and makes things visible. Have you ever thought of God's Word as a light—*a natural agent that stimulates sight and makes things visible?*

When I connected this definition to scripture, it made perfect sense. The darkness I was experiencing felt overwhelming because I wasn't immersing myself in God's Word. Simply put, the light had been turned off.

There are two lights we need to focus on:

1. The **Word of God** as light.
2. Jesus Christ as light.

Both must be activated and applied in our lives. Imagine a room with a light bulb and a switch. The light will never illuminate the room unless the switch is flipped. Similarly, we must take active steps to turn on and keep the light in our lives.

How do we do that? By building a relationship with Christ, immersing ourselves in the Word, living it out, committing to prayer, and submitting to God's will.

EXERCISE:

Commit John 8:12 and Psalm 119:105 to memory. Visualize a light bulb and imagine it filled with the things you need to turn on the light and keep it shining—prayer, studying the Word, worship, community, obedience, etc. Write those things down or draw them inside a light bulb outline.

PRAYER:

Father, I thank You for the light You've placed within me. I confess that I've neglected to activate it, but today I ask for Your help to turn it on and keep it on. Jesus, You are the light, and Your Word is the lamp guiding my path. Forgive me for allowing darkness to take up space in my life. From this day forward, I declare that the light is on. In Jesus Christ's mighty name, Amen.

REFLECTIONS:

_____

_____

_____

_____

_____

_____

_____

_____

_____

_____

_____

_____

_____

_____

_____

_____

_____

_____

_____

DAY 21

KNOW YOUR WEAPONS!

"For the word of God is quick, and powerful, and sharper than any two-edged sword, piercing even to the dividing asunder of soul and spirit, and of the joints and marrow, and is a discerner of the thoughts and intents of the heart."
   - HEBREWS 4:12 (KJV)

"And take the helmet of salvation, and the sword of the Spirit, which is the word of God."
   - EPHESIANS 6:17 (KJV)

DEVOTIONAL:

Do you know your weapons? Imagine being at war, surrounded by weapons, but unable to use them because you don't know anything about them.

Our main weapon is the **Bible**, the Word of God, and it is far more powerful than we often realize. For years, I thought reading a quick scripture was enough, but it wasn't. Hebrews 4:12 reminds us that the Word of God is:

1. **Living**
2. **Powerful**
3. **Sharper than any two-edged sword**

A double-edged sword is designed to cut deeply and effectively with both edges. In scripture, this imagery shows us how God's Word penetrates our souls, exposing our sins and breaking through our excuses.

Not using this weapon—the double-edged sword—leaves us at a disadvantage. The Word is not only for fighting external battles but also for dealing with our internal struggles. These struggles could be thoughts, past experiences, harmful environments, or societal pressures.

The Word of God is truth, and the truth sets us free (John 8:32). Let's commit to knowing and wielding our weapon so we are prepared for every battle—both within and without.

EXERCISE:

Commit Hebrews 4:12 and Ephesians 6:17 to memory. Look up an image of a double-edged sword and visualize its design and power. Then, make a list of scriptures that address the struggles you're facing—whether they are internal or external—and meditate on them.

PRAYER:

Father, I thank You for the gift of Your Word. I acknowledge that it is my most powerful weapon, and I ask for Your forgiveness for not using it as I should. Help me to internalize and apply Your Word daily. Let me hide it in my heart so that I might not sin against You. Prepare me to face every battle, knowing that Your Word equips me for victory. In Jesus' mighty name, Amen.

REFLECTIONS:

_____

_____

_____

_____

_____

_____

_____

_____

_____

_____

_____

_____

_____

_____

_____

_____

_____

_____

DAY 22

ISOLATION SITUATION!

"Where no counsel is, the people fall: but in the multitude of counsellors there is safety."

— PROVERBS 11:14 (KJV)

DEVOTIONAL:

Let me start by saying this is still a work in progress for me—so let's walk through this together.

One thing I've noticed about dealing with depression is how common it is to isolate ourselves. This can happen for many reasons, such as avoiding the need to explain emotions we may not even fully understand. Proverbs 11:14 highlights the importance of counsel, or advice. Yet, if I'm honest, seeking advice was rarely my priority when I was experiencing depression.

Isolation often comes from an inability to communicate what we're feeling. While I'm not suggesting that we share everything with everyone, we *do* need people—even when we feel we don't. We need to ask God to bless us with a community, or as Proverbs puts it, a "multitude of counsellors," where we can feel safe.

Safe counsel, however, isn't a group of people who simply agree with everything we say or feel. Instead, it's about surrounding ourselves with individuals who help guide us toward God's will. Receiving counsel requires humility and a willingness to seek clarity through prayer. It can seem like a lot of effort, but it's necessary for growth and healing.

EXERCISE:

Commit Proverbs 11:14 to memory. Create a list of people you trust and can reach out to during difficult times. Additionally, find a Bible study group at your church or a local assembly and commit to attending weekly for community and support.

PRAYER:

Father, thank You for showing me the importance of godly counsel. I recognize that I've struggled and even failed in some areas because I lacked the wisdom of others. Please reveal the individuals I need to connect with to help me along this journey. Teach me to be humble and open to their guidance. In Jesus' mighty name, Amen.

DONJIA M WALLS

REFLECTIONS:

_____

_____

_____

_____

_____

_____

_____

_____

_____

_____

_____

_____

_____

_____

_____

_____

_____

_____

_____

_____

_____

_____

DAY 23

THE TREASURE

"Lay not up for yourselves treasures upon earth, where moth and rust doth corrupt, and where thieves break through and steal: but lay up for yourselves treasures in heaven, where neither moth nor rust doth corrupt, and where thieves do not break through nor steal: for where your treasure is, there will your heart be also."

— MATTHEW 6:19–21 (KJV)

DEVOTIONAL:

Think about an item you've purchased or been given—something valuable to you. Do you have it in mind? Now, consider how you would feel if that item were lost, stolen, or destroyed.

The word *treasure* can mean a "quantity of valuable objects" (noun) or a "valued item" (verb). Depression can sometimes stem from regret over treasures we've failed to obtain. I remember placing immense value on what others said or did to me. The hardest truth I had to face was this: *The things I valued the most did not value me.*

I had to ask God to help me shift my focus from earthly treasures to heavenly ones. The Bible gives us several ways we can store up "treasures in heaven," including:

- Faithfully enduring persecution (*Matthew 5:11–12; 2 Corinthians 4:16–18; 2 Timothy 4:8*)
- Loving your enemies (*Matthew 5:43–48*)
- Praying in secret (*Matthew 6:5–6*)
- Serving the Lord and His people (*Matthew 10:41–42; 1 Corinthians 3:8; Hebrews 6:10*)

The treasures of heaven are eternal, unlike earthly possessions, which can be destroyed or stolen. Let's ask God to help us value what truly matters.

EXERCISE:

Commit Matthew 6:19–21 to memory. Write down the worldly things you value most and compare them to the heavenly treasures mentioned above. Reflect on how you can realign your priorities.

PRAYER:

In the mighty and matchless name of Jesus Christ, I ask for Your help in understanding that my treasures are not here on earth but are in heaven. Thank You for the many treasures I already have in You. Change my heart wherever I treasure worldly things above heavenly ones. I trust that You can and will do it. Thank You, Jesus. Amen.

REFLECTIONS:

_____

_____

_____

_____

_____

_____

_____

_____

_____

_____

_____

_____

_____

_____

_____

_____

_____

_____

_____

_____

DAY 24
THE CONDEMNATION/DENIAL

"There is therefore now no condemnation to them which are in Christ Jesus, who walk not after the flesh, but after the Spirit."

— ROMANS 8:1 (KJV)

DEVOTIONAL:

Let's get vulnerable. *Condemnation* refers to strong disapproval, and in today's world, it's often tied to the opinions of others. Living in an era dominated by social media—where likes, shares, comments, and cancel culture take center stage—it can be challenging to push past the weight of condemnation.

Romans 8:1 reminds us that in Christ, there is no longer any condemnation. Yet, many of us still take in the disapproval of others and internalize it. This can amplify feelings of depression, especially if we're reliant on people's input, approval, or validation.

I went through a season where I had to log off social media for several months. During that time, I sought God and asked Him to help me break free from my dependency on likes, comments, and recognition. It was through this process that I began to grasp the depth of Jesus' work on the cross.

Acceptance is a major need for many of us. When we don't feel accepted, we often search endlessly to find it. But here's the good news: our Heavenly Father sent His Son to show us what true acceptance and love look like. In Christ, we are fully loved, fully accepted, and fully free.

EXERCISE:

Commit Romans 8:1 to memory. Write down every condemning statement you've heard from others and those you've spoken over yourself or others. Once you're done, rip the paper into as many pieces as you can, symbolizing the destruction of those lies.

PRAYER:

Father, guard my mind and heart from the condemnation I've carried and labeled as truth. Reveal to me every condemning word I've spoken or received. Today, I deny their power over my life and embrace the freedom found in You. In Jesus' mighty name, Amen.

REFLECTIONS:

_____

_____

_____

_____

_____

_____

_____

_____

_____

_____

_____

_____

_____

_____

_____

_____

_____

_____

_____

_____

_____

DAY 25
LET'S BOAST

> "For this thing I besought the Lord thrice, that it might depart from me. And he said unto me, My grace is sufficient for thee: for my strength is made perfect in weakness. Most gladly therefore will I rather glory in my infirmities, that the power of Christ may rest upon me."
>
> — 2 CORINTHIANS 12:8–9 (KJV)

DEVOTIONAL:

Paul's vision in 2 Corinthians 12:1–10 is powerful, but verses 8 and 9 stand out. Often, shame creeps in when we feel that what we're going through is too embarrassing or unworthy to share. Yet Paul gives us a green light to boast in our weaknesses.

Boasting in weakness feels like a strange juxtaposition. Typically, boasting and weakness aren't connected unless someone is mocking another's inability to do something. But God isn't a bully, and His kingdom operates on principles vastly different from the world's.

As mature believers, we must embrace this truth: God does not compete with us. It can't be *our* strength versus His—it has to be our weakness paired with His strength. This concept, though counterintuitive, is central to the gospel. Even the disciples struggled to grasp the paradox of Christ's death as the ultimate display of power through weakness.

This is why our testimonies matter. Sharing your story is a form of boasting about your weaknesses and proclaiming God's strength and glory in your life. This devotional itself is an example of boasting—it's my opportunity to share how God's strength is perfected in my weakness, with the hope that someone else may be encouraged and strengthened.

EXERCISE:

Commit 2 Corinthians 12:8–9 to memory. Reflect on this statement and complete it:

"I boast in the _____ because in it I know God is made strong."

Recite this statement as many times as you need to, especially in moments of doubt or shame.

PRAYER:

Holy Spirit, help me to boast in the areas of my life that I feel ashamed of, and in the things that make me weak. I know that in my weakness, Your strength is perfected. Thank You in advance for what You are doing in and through me. In Jesus' mighty name, Amen.

REFLECTIONS:

_____

_____

_____

_____

_____

_____

_____

_____

_____

_____

_____

_____

_____

_____

_____

_____

_____

_____

_____

_____

_____

DAY 26
RENEW!

"And be not conformed to this world: but be ye transformed by the renewing of your mind, that ye may prove what is that good, and acceptable, and perfect, will of God."

— ROMANS 12:2 (KJV)

DEVOTIONAL:

This scripture required me to break it down.

Conform means "to comply with rules, standards, or laws." Let's insert this definition into the scripture:

"And do not comply with the rules, standards, and laws of this world…."

Often, we conform under the guise of not wanting to "offend" others. However, when we conform, we are disobeying God, who clearly commands us not to do so. Instead, He instructs us to *transform* and *renew* our minds.

Here's the revelation God gave me about renewal: *Renew* means "to resume (an activity) after an interruption." God revealed that He knew the world would teach us things contrary to His truth, causing an "interruption" in the way we think and live. This is why He commands us to renew our minds—to correct what the world has corrupted.

The question is: *How do we transform and renew our minds?*

Here are seven steps I've implemented that help me:

1. Stop waiting for an outside miracle to change my mind.
2. Stop believing that I can't control my thoughts.
3. Understand that what I feed my mind becomes my mindset.
4. Confess what I believe, not what I feel.
5. Resist negative thoughts, assist positive ones.
6. Celebrate the process.
7. Expect change and challenges.

Renewal is a continuous process that allows us to align our minds with God's truth, enabling us to live out His perfect will.

EXERCISE:

Commit Romans 12:2 to memory. Reflect on areas of your mindset that need to be renewed. Write them down and submit them to God in prayer.

PRAYER:

Abba, help me to renew my mind. I've seen, learned, and embraced things that do not align with Your design for me. Forgive me for adopting concepts and ideas that are not from You. Today, I denounce every mindset that is not rooted in Your truth. Transform me through the renewal of my mind. In Jesus' mighty name, Amen!

REFLECTIONS:

_____

_____

_____

_____

_____

_____

_____

_____

_____

_____

_____

_____

_____

_____

_____

_____

_____

_____

_____

DAY 27

DON'T GO BACK, KEEP WORKING!

"Stand fast therefore in the liberty wherewith Christ hath made us free, and be not entangled again with the yoke of bondage."

— GALATIANS 5:1 (KJV)

DEVOTIONAL:

We've reached day 27—what an incredible journey it has been!

What better way to conclude this devotional than with Galatians 5:1? Paul is crystal clear: stand firm in the freedom Christ has given you and don't return to what once enslaved you.

Sometimes, we mistake freedom for being able to do whatever we want. But that kind of living doesn't lead to true freedom—it often enslaves us to our own desires. After these 27 days, we cannot go back! We've gained too much wisdom and insight to return to life as it was before.

True freedom is found in Jesus, in God's Word, and in following Him wholeheartedly. Freedom is found when we live in the purpose God created us for. This is the freedom Paul calls his readers to embrace.

Let's commit to moving forward, holding on to the truths we've learned and the tools we've gained. As mentioned at the start of this journey, this devotional is a resource. Just because we've reached the end doesn't mean we can't revisit it when we need a refresher or encouragement.

EXERCISE:

Commit Galatians 5:1 to memory. Schedule a time to revisit this devotional in the future to refresh your mind on the lessons and tools you've gained.

PRAYER:

Father, thank You for bringing me to this point in my journey. I'm grateful for all I've learned and for everything You've done in me through this devotional. Help me to retain and use the tools and weapons I've obtained. Strengthen me to stand firm in the freedom You've given me and never return to bondage. In Jesus' mighty name, Amen!

DONJIA M WALLS

REFLECTIONS:

_____

_____

_____

_____

_____

_____

_____

_____

_____

_____

_____

_____

_____

_____

_____

_____

_____

_____

_____

_____

_____

_____

ABOUT THE AUTHOR

Donjia M. Walls was born in 1990 in Newark, New Jersey. She was raised in East Orange, New Jersey, and later returned to Newark in 2009 at the age of 18. Donjia holds an Associate of Arts in Early Childhood Education, a Bachelor of Arts in Sociology, and a Post-Baccalaureate Certificate in Prejudice Reduction and Teaching the History of the Holocaust.

Donjia is a devoted wife and mother, a Behavior Assistant, an event and wedding coordinator, a youth leader with over ten years of experience, a recording artist, and an author. Her previous work includes *The Path 2 Take*, a youth and young adult Christian fiction novel.

With a charge from the Holy Spirit to bring hope, healing, and deliverance to those in need, Donjia reflects this mission in all her writings, using her gifts to inspire and uplift others.

facebook.com/donjia.wilson.3
instagram.com/d.m.walls